COWS

A TRUE BOOK

by

Sara Swan Miller

Children's Press®
A Division of Grolier Publishing
New York London Hong Kong Sydney
Danbury, Connecticut

Reading Consultant
Linda Cornwell
*Coordinator of School Quality
and Professional Improvement
Indiana State Teachers Association*

Content Consultant
Jan Jenner

Cows help steady
a newborn calf.

Visit Children's Press® on the Internet at:
http://publishing.grolier.com

Library of Congress Cataloging-in-Publication Data

Miller, Sara Swan
    Cows / by Sara Swan Miller.
        p. cm. — (A True book)
    Includes bibliographical references and index.
    Summary: Describes the physical traits, lifestyle, and behavior of cows,
with an emphasis on dairy cows and their role in providing humans with
milk.
    ISBN 0-516-21577-9 (lib. bdg.)   0-516-27181-4 (pbk.)
    1. Dairy cattle Juvenile literature.   2. Cows   Juvenile literature.
    [1. Dairy cattle. 2. Cows.] I. Title. II. Series.
SF208.M565   2000
636. 2' 142—dc21   99-30138
                                                         CIP

Contents

States where the most cows are found include California, Wisconsin, Minnesota, and New York.

The Cow Story

If someone asked you to name a farm animal, what would you say? Would you think of a cow first? Take a ride in the country and you'll see, and hear, plenty of cows. These are dairy cows. They're the cows farmers raise for their milk.

People started keeping cows more than six thousand years ago in Asia. Before that, people hunted them for meat, hide, and horns. Then people began feeding and taming the cows. That way, they wouldn't have to hunt them. They could settle down to raise food and animals.

After a while, people began using cows to pull and carry loads and to help them plow fields. Finally, they realized they could use their milk, too.

This wall painting shows farmers in ancient Egypt using cows for plowing.

A present-day farmer and his cows in Tibet.

Now there are cows all over the world. They are gentle, patient animals. There are other dairy animals, too.

Goats and sheep also give milk. But cows make more milk than all the other dairy animals.

This farmer in Italy is milking a goat.

A Highland cow and calf in Scotland

Farmers saw that some cows gave more milk than others. Some cows' milk was richer, or better tasting. They would mate the best cows with the best bulls to make the best calves. Over thousands of years, people made many different breeds, or kinds, of cows this way.

Now there are more than 270 breeds of cows. More than 180 breeds are dairy cows. Dairy farmers choose to raise the breed of cow that suits them best.

This Longhorn cow and calf live on a Wisconsin dairy farm.

Sacred Cows

The cows of India are called zebus (ZEE-booz). The Hindus who live there believe that cows are sacred animals. They will drink a cow's milk, but they will not kill one for meat. Zebus wander freely through the villages and even the big cities. People leave food as they pass by for the cows to eat. Sometimes the zebus help themselves to food in the open-air vegetable markets.

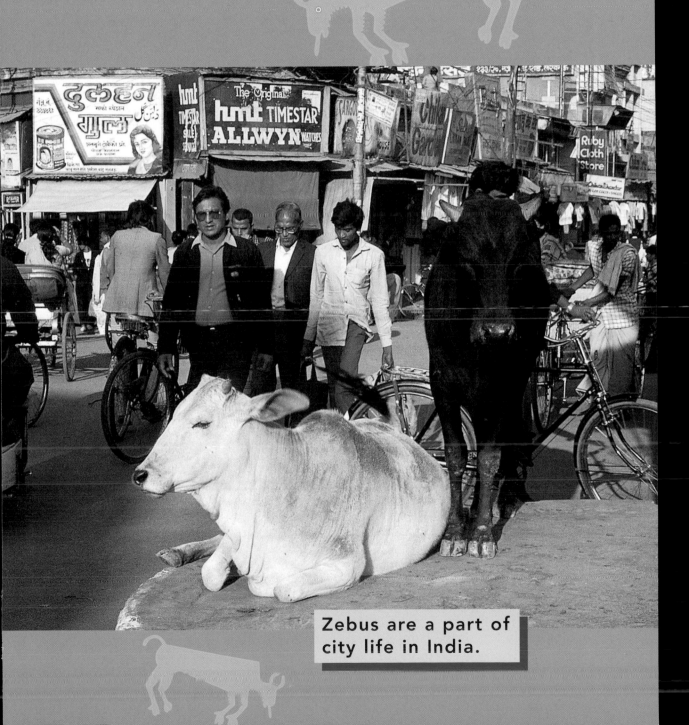

Zebus are a part of city life in India.

A Holstein-Friesian cow

Some Favorite Cow Breeds

In the United States, most of the cows you'll see on dairy farms are Holstein-Friesians (HOLE-steen-FREE-zhunz). They make a lot of milk. Jersey cows are another common breed. They don't give as much milk. But their milk is rich in butterfat.

A Jersey cow

In places where the grass is
poor, people raise Ayrshires
(AIR-shers). They can survive
on less food than other cows.
The white-and-golden-brown
Guernsey (GERN-zee) make

A Guernsey cow

Like the Brown Swiss cow, the Simmental cow comes from Switzerland.

less milk than Ayrshires. But the milk has more butterfat. Brown Swiss cows come from the mountains of Switzerland. Their milk is made into Swiss cheese.

A cow lies in the grass to chew its cud.

What Are Cows Like?

Have you seen cows lying in a field chewing? It looks as though they're chewing huge wads of gum. They're really chewing their cud.

Grass is hard to digest, so a cow has a special stomach. It has four parts. When a cow eats grass, it chews the grass

Cows have a strong set of lower teeth to help them chew grass and rough plants.

only enough to make it wet. The grass goes down into the first two parts of the stomach. The cow keeps eating until it's full. Then it lies down and brings up the wad of grass. The cow chews its cud well this time. Then the cud goes down into the third and fourth parts of its stomach. There the cud is digested.

Cows spend about eight hours a day eating. Their mouth is well suited for eating

Special feeding containers called troughs hold hay for the cows to eat.

grass. Instead of teeth, they have a tough pad on the front of the top part of their mouth. On the bottom of their mouth they have eight teeth in front for tearing off grass. Then they grind it with their twenty-four back teeth, called molars.

In the winter, the farmer brings the cows into the barn. There they eat a mix of hay, corn, barley, grass, and cotton

In winter, cows spend more time inside the barn.

seed. They even get cereal left over from factories that make breakfast cereal. Cows eat as much as 80 pounds (36 kg) of food a day. They drink 30 to 40 gallons (114–151 liters) of water each day, too.

Cows don't make milk until they have a calf. Cows can give birth when they're about two years old. They carry their calf for nine months until it's born. When the calf is only about an hour old, it is already

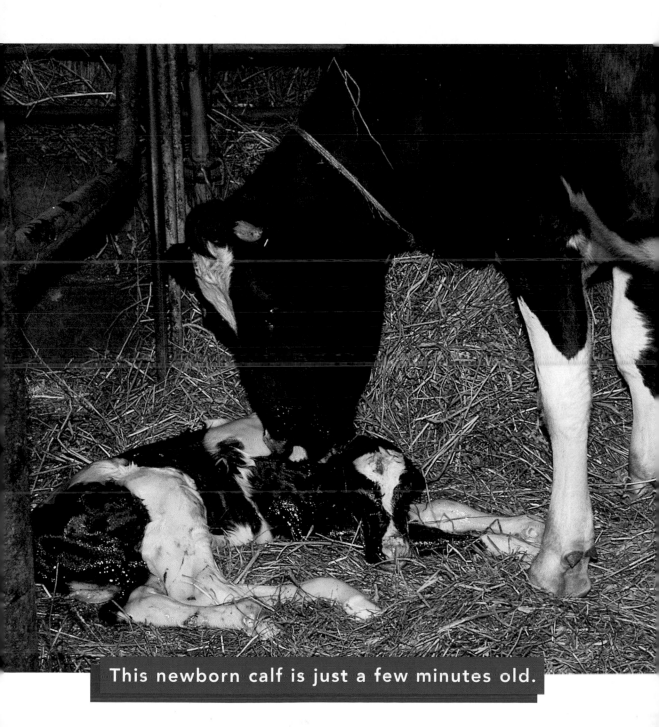
This newborn calf is just a few minutes old.

A newborn calf drinks its mother's milk (right) then later uses a bottle feeder.

standing and drinking its mother's milk.

After a few days, the farmer takes the calf away from its mother and feeds it milk—from a bottle or a pail. The calf doesn't need all the milk its mother makes. The farmer milks out the rest. This is the milk that people use.

The mother continues to make milk for many months. The more food it eats, the more milk it produces. Most

Dairy farms have areas where cows wait to give birth.

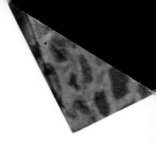

cows give about 5 gallons (19 L) a day. But some give as much as 8 gallons (30 L).

Two months before the cow is going to have its next calf, the farmer stops milking it. The cow stops making milk. This is known as being dry. The farmer feeds the cow a lot of food to help it get fat and healthy before its next calf is born. Then it will start making milk again.

This woman milks a cow in the English countryside more than fifty years ago.

Life on a Dairy Farm

Long ago, most people lived on farms. They kept just a few cows. They would milk the cows by hand. They made their own butter and cheese. Sometimes they had too much milk for their family. They would sell the rest to their neighbors.

Milk is ready for transport in this refrigerated truck.

Milk spoiled too easily for farmers to send it far from the farm. When refrigeration was invented, everything changed. Today, farmers send the milk to dairy plants in refrigerated trucks. There it's made ready for market.

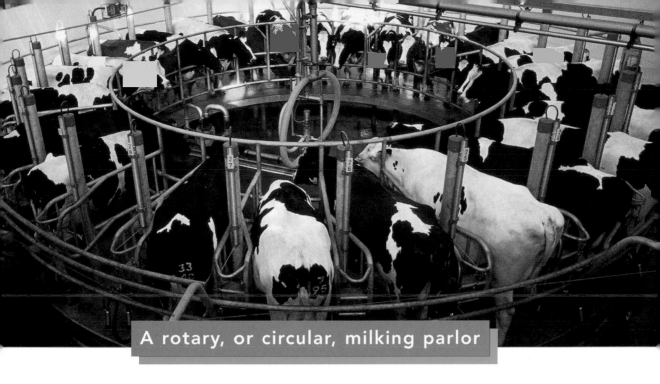

A rotary, or circular, milking parlor

Dairy farmers still have to work very hard. They get up early to milk their herd. First, they bring the cows into a building called a milking parlor. Then they put the cows in special stalls, which keep them still. Having food to eat also helps keep the cows from moving about. Next, the farmers wash off the cows' udders so that dirt and germs won't get into the milk. Finally, the farmers hook up the cows to milking machines. The milk travels in tubes to a storage tank to stay cool. Later, a dairy truck will pick it up and take it to a dairy factory.

But the work has just begun. Dairy farmers have to keep records of how much

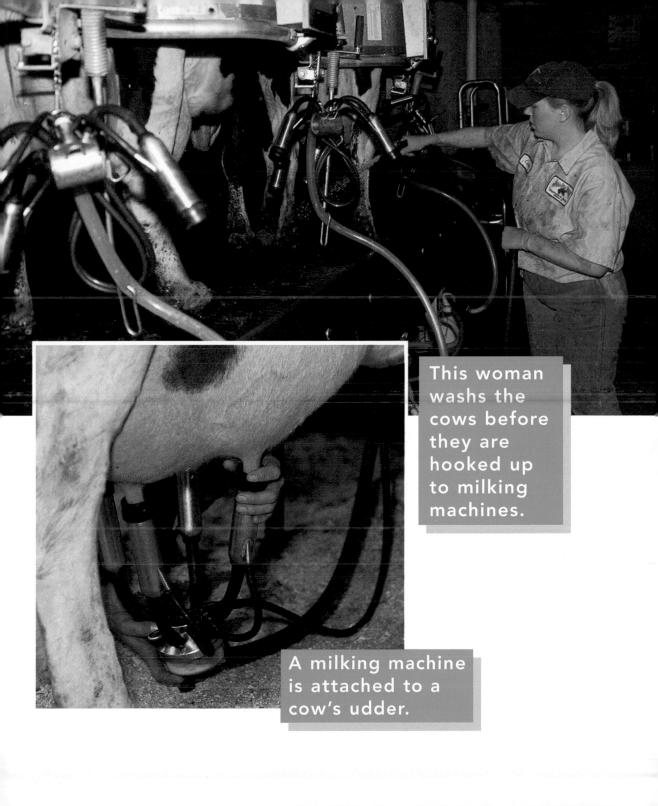

This woman washs the cows before they are hooked up to milking machines.

A milking machine is attached to a cow's udder.

A vet gives this calf a checkup.

milk each cow gives. If a cow isn't giving much, it may be sick. Dairy farmers check their herds each day to be sure all the cows are healthy.

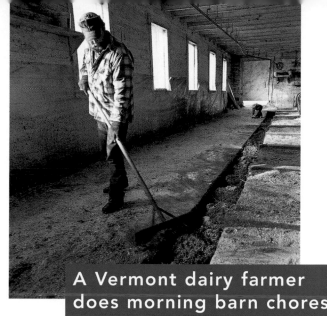

A Vermont dairy farmer does morning barn chores.

In the winter, the next thing to do is to clean out all the stalls. Farmers have to rake out the dirty straw and put down clean straw. Depending on the size of the herd, this can take a long time! The cows need to be cleaned, too. Dirty cows can catch diseases.

Of course, the cows need to be fed. They may get as many as eight meals a day. Finally, at the end of the day, all the cows need to be milked again.

In the summer, the cows live in a pasture. There are no stalls to be cleaned. But the farmers still have plenty of work to do. They have to repair the fences around the herd. Cows can get hurt if they step on broken fencing. Farmers also have to grow hay for the winter and

A Limousin cow and calf have plenty of grass to eat in this pasture.

mow it when it's ready. And they still have to milk the cows twice a day.

Dairy farmers need to work hard every day of the year. But having contented, healthy cows giving good milk is worth it.

More than Milk

Milk is more than just a good drink. People make many other foods from it. The cream that rises to the top can be made into whipped cream, sour cream, and cream cheese. Cheese, cottage cheese, butter, buttermilk, and yogurt are all made from milk.

Which ice cream treat would you choose?

Most people's favorite food from milk is ice cream!

Look in your refrigerator. How many foods there are made from milk?

Make Your Own Butter

Using a home butter churn long ago

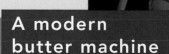

A modern butter machine

It's fun to make a little butter by yourself.

- Fill a small glass jar half full with heavy cream. Then start shaking it. You may want to get a few friends to help you shake. It takes a while, and your hand may get tired.
- Keep shaking until you have a solid clump of butter. The thin liquid left behind is called buttermilk. Many people like to drink it.
- Pour the buttermilk into a glass. Then put the butter in a bowl. You may want to mix a little salt into the butter. Now spread it on a cracker. Fresh butter is delicious, isn't it? Thank the cows for it!

To Find Out More

Here are some additional resources to help you learn more about cows:

 **Books**

Aliki. **Milk: From Cow to Carton.** HarperCollins, 1992.

Jeunesse, Gallimard. **Farm Animals.** Scholastic, 1998.

Kalman, Bobbie. **Hooray for Dairy Farming!** Crabtree Pub., 1997.

Ling, Mary. **See How They Grow: Calf.** DK Publishing, 1993.

Older, Jules and Lyn Severance. **Cow.** Charlesbridge, 1997.

Radtke, Becky. **Farm Activity Book.** Dover Publications, 1997.

Webster, Charlie. **Farm Animals.** Barron's, 1997.

Organizations and Online Sites

Breeds of Livestock
http://www.ansi.okstate.edu/BREEDS/cattle

If you want to see pictures of many different breeds of cattle and descriptions of each, this is the site to visit.

Information Dirt Road
http://www.ics.uci.edu/~pazzani/4H/InfoDirt.html

This site contains information on raising different kinds of farm animals, including cows.

Kids Farm
http://www.kidsfarm.com

Kids Farm is a lot of fun and educational, too. It is created by people who run a farm in the Colorado Rocky Mountains and brings you real sights and sounds of animals on the farm.

Moomilk
http://www.moomilk.com

You can learn a lot about the dairy industry at this site. There is a virtual tour, information about cows and milk, and games and contests.

National 4-H Council
http://www.fourhcouncil.edu

This site will tell you about animal clubs and special interest activities for youth across the United States.

Important Words

butterfat the natural fat in milk, which can be made into butter

contented happy and satisfied

refrigeration the means to keep food from spoiling by keeping it cold

sacred holy, deserving great respect

stall a section in a stable or barn where a single animal is kept

taming taking from a wild or natural state and training to live with or be useful to people

udder the baglike part of a cow that hangs down near its back legs, it contains the glands that produce milk

Index

Meet the Author

Sara Swan Miller has enjoyed working with children all her life, first as a nursery-school teacher, and later as an outdoor environmental educator at the Mohonk Preserve in New Paltz, New York. Now Ms. Miller is a full-time writer. She has written more than thirty books for children, including *Chickens*, *Goats*, *Pigs*, and *Sheep*, in the True Books series.